IMAGES
of America

HOPATCONG
A CENTURY OF MEMORIES

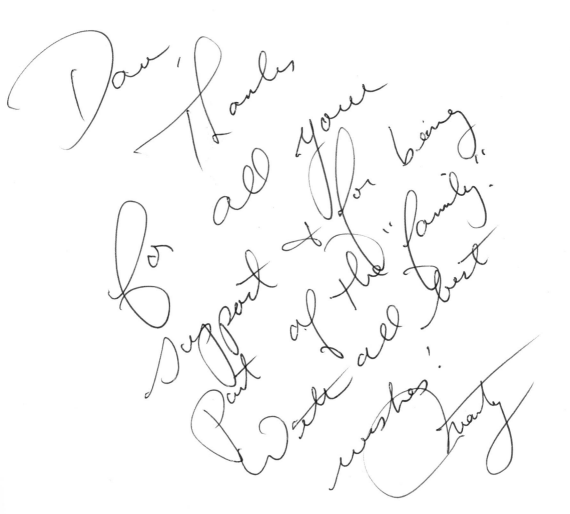

Dan,
Thanks for all your support + for being part of the "family".
Best all best wishes!
Tracy

An aerial view of Hopatcong and its surrounding environs in 1955.

IMAGES
of America

HOPATCONG
A CENTURY OF MEMORIES

Martin Kane

ARCADIA

Published by Arcadia Publishing,
an imprint of Tempus Publishing, Inc.
2 Cumberland Street
Charleston, SC 29401

Printed in Great Britain.

Library of Congress Catalog Card Number: 98-85865

For all general information contact Arcadia Publishing at:
Telephone 843-853-2070
Fax 843-853-0044
E-Mail arcadia@charleston.net

For customer service and orders:
Toll-Free 1-888-313-BOOK

Visit us on the internet at http://www.arcadiaimages.com

Hopatcong was "hopping," as seen by this water carnival in Northwood during the late 1940s.

Contents

The author discusses Hopatcong history in River Styx during the summer of 1956.

Acknowledgments

This book would not have been possible if not for the wonderful photographic collection of the Lake Hopatcong Historical Museum. To the hundreds of people who have donated photographs or allowed their photographs to be copied by the Museum, I offer my sincere thanks. I wish I could list all of you individually. Your generosity has ensured that the history of Lake Hopatcong is documented and preserved.

I must also acknowledge the *Lake Hopatcong Breeze*. This publication served the role of Lake Hopatcong's newspaper, faithfully reporting on summer life, from 1894 through 1950, and somewhat less regularly through 1982. Life at the Lake was forever captured and preserved thanks to the *Breeze*.

Special thanks to Rich Willis and Lorraine Lees for allowing their personal photographic collections to be used and for their advice and guidance throughout this project. Also, special thanks to Hopatcong Mayor Cliff Lundin and to Barbara Rossy Jones, for their advice, special knowledge, and love for the Borough.

Thanks to my mom and dad who first brought me to River Styx at seven months of age and enabled me to spend my summers growing up at the Lake. I only wish my father, who deeply loved the Lake, could have lived to see this book in print.

My deepest thanks to my family. Thanks to Lucky for guarding the manuscript. Thanks to Natalie for trying to understand what her dad was doing and for supplying many delightful distractions along the way. And most of all thanks to my best friend and wife, Laurie—her ideas were invaluable and the long hours she spent helping choose photographs and editing the text made this book possible.

Hopefully, this book will bring the same enjoyment to the reader as its creation has brought to the writer.

Things looked a bit different than today in the River Styx of 1908.

Introduction

The history of the Borough of Hopatcong parallels the history of the Lake—from its emergence as a great hotel resort, to its evolution into a summer community similar to the Jersey shore, and its eventual transformation into an all-year-round community. The first 100 years were filled with excitement—from the hotels, to the night life, to the "rich and famous" who visited and made Hopatcong their home. It is a history of both progress and missed opportunities, of foresight and lack of vision. While Hopatcong will never return to the days that were, the next 100 years will present many challenges. Hopefully, the future will see us learn from the past and work to keep Hopatcong a special place. Bring on the first 100 years . . .

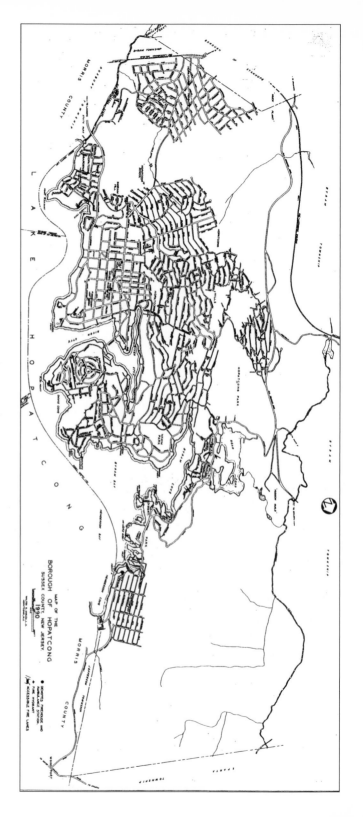

Map of present-day Hopatcong.

One
Welcome to Brooklyn

LAKE HOPATCONG HOUSE, AT LAKE HOPATCONG, NOW OPEN.

Gentlemen with their families, or single gentlemen, can make arrangements for Summer Board at reasonable prices. Parties wishing that rare amusement, viz.: "GOOD FISHING," can enjoy it at this beautiful place to perfection; also, GOOD BATHING. It is two-and-a-half hours' ride from New York, by Morris and Essex Railroad to Drakeville station, where stages will be in waiting to convey passengers to the House, a distance of three miles. Post Office address—Drakeville, Morris county, N. J.   J. H. DAVIS.

Prior to direct rail service in the 1880s, Lake Hopatcong was a destination for the more adventuresome, as indicated by this advertisement from the August 6, 1859 issue of *Harper's Weekly*. After a two-and-one-half-hour train ride, passengers had to disembark at Drakesville (now known as Ledgewood) and take a stagecoach over dirt roads to their destination. The Lake Hopatcong House was located on what is today Lakeside Boulevard. It would later be known as simply the Hopatcong House.

Hopatcong has never had its own railroad station. Passengers traveling to Hopatcong in the early years either took the Central Railroad of New Jersey to Nolans Point or the Lackawanna Railroad to Landing. Steamboats met arriving trains and transported passengers to their destinations around the Lake. In this *c.* 1900 photograph, arriving passengers disembark a Central Railroad of New Jersey train at Nolans Point.

The Morris and Essex Railroad, later acquired by the Lackawanna Railroad, preceded the Central Railroad in reaching Lake Hopatcong. Tracks were laid through Landing in the 1850s, but as there was no station, arriving passengers had to disembark at Drakesville (now Ledgewood). A station was finally built at Landing in the 1880s. In this *c.* 1910 photograph, a steamboat waits on the Morris Canal in Landing for a train to arrive.

Lake Hopatcong
and THE SUSSEX HILLS

The Lake's two railroads heavily promoted Lake Hopatcong in the late 19th and early 20th centuries. Although the Lackawanna Railroad only constructed a station at Landing after the Central Railroad was enjoying success with its service to Nolans Point, it became the predominant rail link to Lake Hopatcong in the 1920s and 1930s.

The Morris Canal was a major factor in Lake Hopatcong's development. Stretching across northern New Jersey, the canal connected the Delaware and Hudson Rivers from the 1830s until its abandonment in 1924. Lake Hopatcong was its largest single source of water. This c. 1910 photograph shows lock tender Rube Messinger manning the canal lock, which was located at what is now Hopatcong State Park.

As a 19th-century "highway" across New Jersey, the Morris Canal was a major source of commerce. At Lake Hopatcong, iron ore was brought by wagon, and later rail, from mines in Jefferson Township and loaded onto canal boats. The boats were then towed across the Lake by steamboat to the canal lock. From here, horses or mules would furnish the power along the canal. Thanks to business from the canal, a small community, which became known as Brooklyn, developed around the canal lock. This c. 1905 photograph shows a typical canal boat on the Morris Canal.

Early development at Lake Hopatcong tended to be along the eastern shore. Dominated by hilly terrain and poor access, the western shore of the Lake was slower to develop. This began to change as cottages were built north of River Styx in the 1880s and 1890s. This c. 1900 photograph shows the unpaved road north of River Styx.

As the western shore of Lake Hopatcong began to develop, landowners believed they were not receiving sufficient attention and resources from Byram Township. For the western shore to properly develop, the residents concluded they needed to break from Byram Township and establish their own municipality. On April 2, 1898, the New Jersey Legislature approved the formation of the Borough of Brooklyn. With a voting population of 43, the Borough of Brooklyn held its first elections on May 4, 1898.

May 4th 1898

BOROUGH OF BROOKLYN,
Sussex County,
New Jersey.

CITIZENS' TICKET.

For Mayor,
RICHARD L. EDWARDS.

For Councilmen,
THEODORE A. K. GESSLER.
JOHN INGRAM.
JOHN ALDRED.
DWIGHT B. SMITH.
LEWIS S. PILCHER.
RICHARD R. SUTTON.

For Justice of the Peace,
GUSTAVE REINBERG.

For Assessor,
THEODORE W. GOBLE.

For Collector,
JOSEPH COCKS.

For Commissioners of Appeals,
ALFRED RAUCHFUSS.
FERDINAND MÜLLER.
BENJAMIN K. ATNO.

For Borough and Poor Money, $50.
For Roads and Streets, $350.

Resolved, that the license money due and received by the Borough shall be expended by the Councilmen as they may deem proper for the benefit of the Borough, with the consent of the mayor.

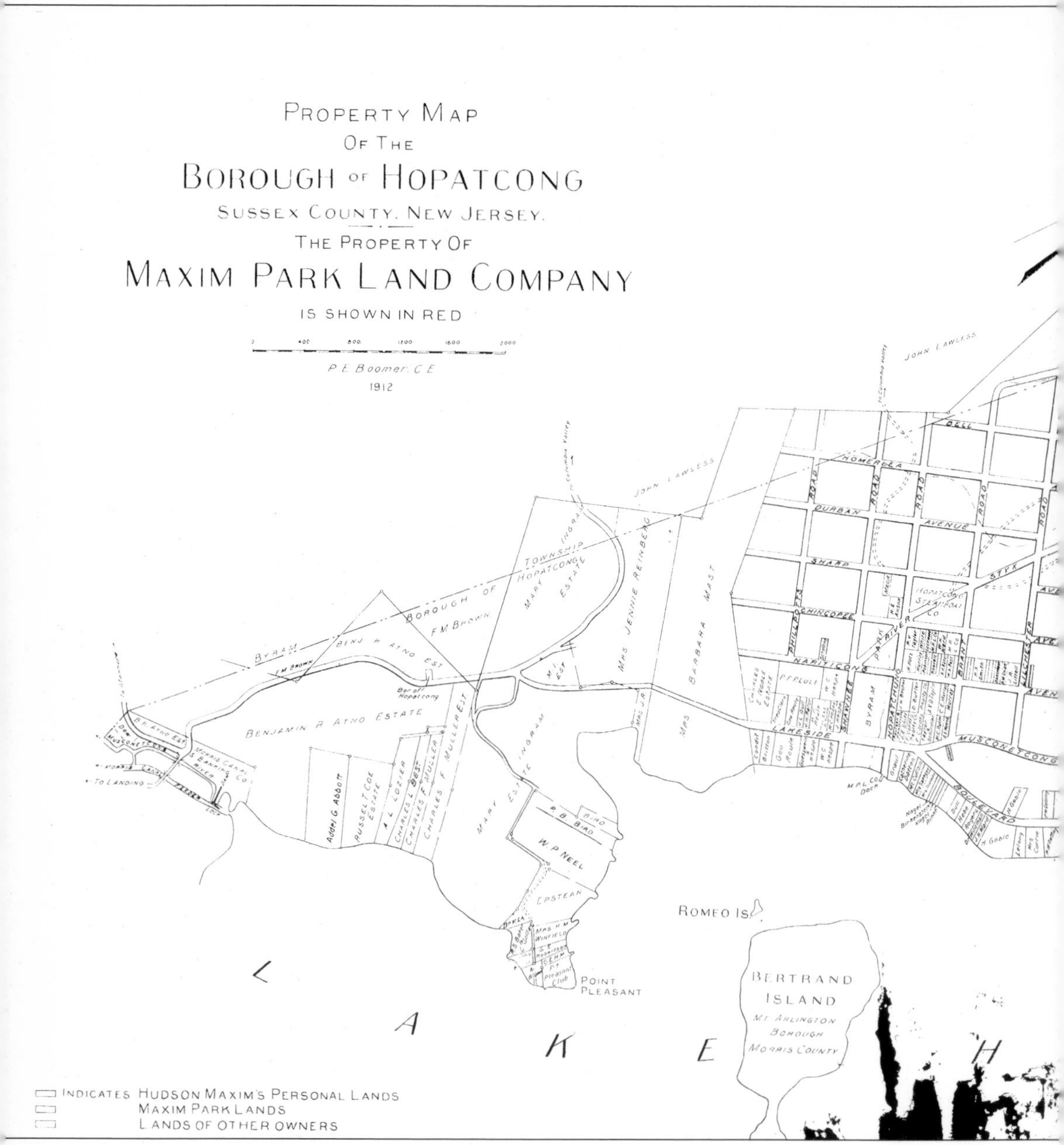

PROPERTY MAP
OF THE
BOROUGH OF HOPATCONG
SUSSEX COUNTY, NEW JERSEY.
THE PROPERTY OF
MAXIM PARK LAND COMPANY
IS SHOWN IN RED
P. E. Boomer, C. E.
1912
ROMEO IS.
BERTRAND ISLAND
MT ARLINGTON BOROUGH
MORRIS COUNTY
POINT PLEASANT
L A K E H
INDICATES HUDSON MAXIM'S PERSONAL LANDS
MAXIM PARK LANDS
LANDS OF OTHER OWNERS

The newly formed Borough stretched from the Musconetcong River, in what is today Hopatcong State Park, to the southern shore of Byram Cove. It was a fairly narrow municipality, created to incorporate the developing lake front properties. This map, prepared for a land development company in 1912, shows the Borough's early boundaries. This left the

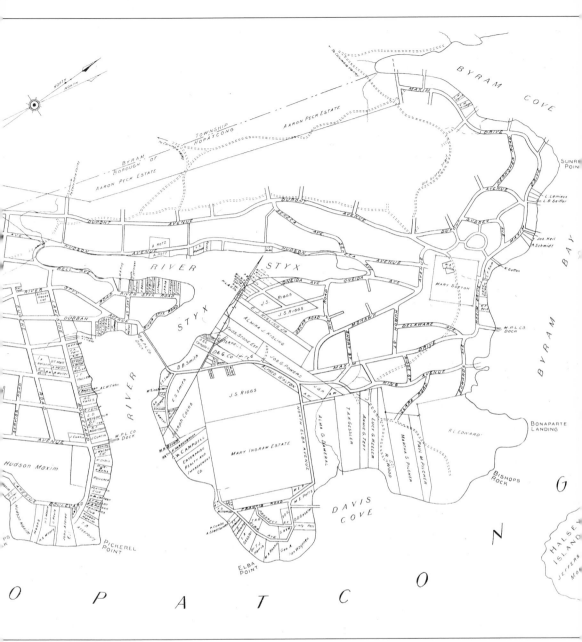

areas of Byram Cove and Northwood, as well as significant lands to the west (including Bear Pond), still in Byram Township. As these locales began to develop, their residents wished to join Hopatcong, which had shared interests. In 1922, the local population of these areas voted to join Hopatcong and the Borough grew to the borders we know today.

1901.
BOROUGH OF BROOKLYN.

For Mayor,

R. L. EDWARDS.

For Councilmen,

THEO. A. K. GESSLER, }
JOHN ALDRED, } *to serve three years.*

For Commissioner of Appeals,

BENJAMIN K. ATNO, *to serve three years.*

For Freeholder,

APPROPRIATIONS RECOMMENDED :

For Borough Expenses, - - $250
" Board of Health, - - - 100
" Poor, - - - - - 50
" Bounty on Foxes per head, - 1

The following Resolutions are also recommended :

Resolved, That the Mayor and Council be and are hereby authorized to appropriate and expend any surplus funds now in the hands of the Treasurer of the Borough, and any available funds that the Treasurer may have or shall receive from the taxes of the years 1900 and 1901 not otherwise appropriated for the purpose of completing payments due on the newly macadamized road and the further improvements of roads within the Borough.

Resolved, Further, That the Mayor and Council be and are hereby authorized to borrow the sum of twelve hundred dollars for the purpose of meeting the indebtedness already incurred in constructing the macadam road from Musconettcong River Bridge to Hopatcong House premises.

The name Brooklyn stemmed from the forge located on land which is now Hopatcong State Park. The Brookland Forge was built around 1750 and operated for about 30 years, utilizing the power generated by the flow of the Musconetcong River as it left Lake Hopatcong. The earth dam constructed by the forge raised the level of Lake Hopatcong approximately 6 feet. During this period, the Lake was referred to either as Great Pond or Brookland Pond. As part of the construction of the Morris Canal in the 1820s, a new dam was installed which raised the Lake another 6 feet. The Lake, now some 12 feet higher than its natural state, became known as Lake Hopatcong. The area around the Morris Canal continued to be called Brookland, although the forge was long gone. In the course of the 19th century, the name was corrupted to Brooklyn, probably due to its more famous namesake. Brooklyn was the obvious choice for the new borough's name. With an annual budget of $400, plus a small amount held in reserve as a bounty for foxes, the Borough entered the 20th century having just completed its first macadamized road. Stretching from Brooklyn-Stanhope Road to Cove Road, the road we know today as Lakeside Boulevard left the Borough $1,200 in debt.

At the time of its incorporation, Brooklyn had three hotels, no churches, and the nearest store was in Landing. The Borough was rural in character, and the hilly terrain supported several farms. In this *c.* 1903 photo, several cows graze by the shore of the Lake with Gustave Reinberg's cottage, Oldfield, dominating the hill in front of Brooklyn Mountain Road.

Brooklyn Mountain Road was already in existence at the time the Borough was incorporated. While it would remain unpaved for many years, it was the main road to Columbia Valley (and to what is now Stanhope-Sparta Road). Even today, Brooklyn Mountain Road remains paved only as far as Columbia Trail. This photo shows Brooklyn Mountain Road in 1899.

17

This 1911 photograph demonstrates the remoteness of Byram Cove. The tree for which Pine Tree Point was named is clearly visible at the shoreline. It was because of this solitude that a Boy Scout camp would be built in this area. In the late 19th and early 20th centuries, a popular day trip involved rowing to the shores of Byram Cove, beaching the boat, and setting off through the woods for a picnic lunch at Bear Pond.

Early life in Brooklyn was centered around the Lake. In an era before air conditioning, Lake Hopatcong offered a cool respite from the cities to the east. Located 914 feet above sea level and fed by natural springs, the Lake quickly began to develop as a resort. This c. 1910 photograph of the Shotwell family captures early life at Sperry Springs.

There really was a Sperry Spring, and it was considered the most celebrated spring at the Lake. Picnic parties heading for Byram Bay or Bear Pond would generally stop to fill their pails at the spring. This *c*. 1908 photograph serves as a testament to the water.

In the Borough's early years, only a few families were year-round residents. One such family was the Sutton family. They had a farm in Sperry Springs and were the only residents of this area when Brooklyn was created. While not set up as a rooming house, boarders were regularly accepted at their farm. Many Sutton descendants reside in the area today.

Like most of the west shore, River Styx was mainly wooded when Brooklyn became a borough. This c. 1900 photograph demonstrates the solitude of this area compared to the "building boom" which was then underway at Mount Arlington and Nolans Point.

This c. 1900 photograph was taken from the dock of the Ithanell Hotel looking west into River Styx Cove. The shoreline on the left is today's Lakeside Boulevard, just before the Hudson Maxim School. As the 20th century dawned, cottages and hotels would soon dot this shoreline.

Two

A Borough by Any Other Name

The newly incorporated Borough soon found that people were confused by the name Brooklyn. The last thing that fledgling hotels and developers needed was confusion as to the name and location of the community. In 1901, the Borough changed its name to Hopatcong. The early campers in this c. 1905 photograph, taken near the present-day Hopatcong State Park, appear that they would have been unconcerned no matter what the Borough was called.

While most working people in America of the late 19th century could not afford more than a day at a resort such as Lake Hopatcong, there was a developing middle class that was beginning to have the time and money for leisure activities and vacations. Camping was a popular alternative to hotels. This 1887 photograph shows an early campsite on Sharp's Rock.

Camping offered the cheapest option for a vacation—all that was needed was a piece of ground and a tent. Many individuals rented land and pitched a tent for a week or more at a time. This 1913 photograph was taken at Robbinwood, campsite of the Robbins family, at the mouth of Mountain Inlet.

Camps attracted many groups, such as college fraternities, which joined together to rent land and set up a more organized campsite. Many of these camps would return to the same site year after year. This *c.* 1920 photograph shows Camp Flash, located on West River Styx Road.

Many campers eventually purchased their campsite and built cottages on the land. This *c.* 1905 photograph shows a tent on a pre-erected wooden floor (which made life a little more comfortable). This tent, located on the Forest Club's property on Lakeside Boulevard almost directly across from the Lake Hopatcong Yacht Club, would soon give way to a cottage.

If George Washington is considered the "father" of the United States, R.L. Edwards can be considered the "father" of Hopatcong. A Wall Street banker who became president of the Bank of the State of New York, Edwards first summered at the Lake in 1875. He became enchanted with the area and purchased a 60-acre tract on the west shore, which encompassed Bishops Rock and Bonaparte Landing. His cottage, Wildwood, was one of only four houses on the west shore when he built it in 1878.

To facilitate access to Wildwood, Edwards constructed a 7-mile wagon road from Landing at his own expense. As others began to build cottages on the west shore, Edwards became a leader in the effort to create a separate municipality. Although a New Yorker for most of the year, Edwards registered as a Brooklyn voter, was elected its first mayor, and held the position for the next 18 years. In this *c.* 1920 photograph, R.L. Edwards and family pose in front of Wildwood.

24

R.L. Edwards was an active boater and driving force in the formation of the Lake Hopatcong Yacht Club. From its formation in 1905 until its clubhouse was completed on Bertrand Island in 1910, club events and meetings were held at Wildwood, as documented by this *c.* 1908 photograph. Edwards continued to summer at Wildwood until his death in 1926. His beloved Wildwood would be sold and developed as Wildwood Park in 1934. In 1940, the name was changed to Wildwood Shores, and the area retains this name today.

The first cottage believed to have been built on the west shore in what is now Hopatcong was Tangle Wild, the summer home of Rev. Dr. T.A.K. Gessler and family. Built in the 1870s, the home (seen in this 1899 photograph) was in the middle of Davis Cove, which has also been known as Gessler Cove. For many years, Dr. Gessler held religious services at his home or at the end of his dock where the congregation sat in canoes, rowboats, or launches. His son Theodore was the second mayor of Hopatcong.

At the turn of the century a summer residence was called a "cottage" whether it had 3 or 30 rooms. The cottage owners behind the drive for Brooklyn's separation from Byram were affluent, and the cottages they built reflected this wealth. One such cottage was Katrina in Davis Cove, built by the Drake family. This c. 1910 photograph shows the boathouse (which still stands) built in 1895 and the main house on the hill.

Next door to Katrina in Davis Cove is Eagle's Nest, seen at the extreme right of this c. 1910 photograph. Constructed high up the mountain, it was built in 1903 by Dr. Lewis S. Pilcher, a prominent early surgeon from Brooklyn, New York, who pioneered many advances in surgery. Dr. Pilcher first came to the Lake in 1878 and spent the next 56 summers here. His beloved Eagle's Nest still overlooks the Lake from high above.

On the opposite shore of Davis Cove, visible on the right side of this 1910 photograph, is Boulders, the cottage of Mr. and Mrs. Dudley Gessler. Built *c.* 1903, it derived its name from the huge gray stones which were quarried from the grounds and used in its construction. Gessler's father, Rev. Dr. T.A.K Gessler, was the next-door neighbor at Tangle Wild.

Located between Elba Point and Davis Cove, Castle Sans Souci was constructed by Dr. and Mrs. George Van Wagonen in 1895. Dr. Van Wagonen, one of the founders of Prudential Insurance, built his cottage of stones from the property to resemble an old turreted castle. This *c.* 1908 photograph shows the boathouse, built in 1905 The main house survives today, but has been so expanded one must be inside to see the original stone walls. The boathouse was demolished in the 1950s.

Located directly on Point Pleasant, the Point Pleasant Club was organized by members of a Newark, New Jersey church in 1888. After a short period of camping, seven cottages were built on the campsite. The club existed into the 1960s and the last of the original cottages survived until the 1970s.

Between Point Pleasant and Ingram Cove, there were two cottages built around 1890, C.O. Brown's Bella Vista and O.F. Megie's Camelot. After the Megie's sold to the Bird family, the cottage was renamed Bird's Nest. This c. 1912 photograph shows the Bird's Nest boathouse. In later years, the upper floor was removed and used elsewhere on the property. The lower floor survives today as a boathouse.

Built by Gustave Reinberg, Oldfield dominated the hill above Lakeside Boulevard. The building lower on the hill was the barn. The property, as seen in this *c.* 1905 photograph, would stay in the Reinberg family into the 1930s. In the late 1930s, it was rented to American Airways as a clubhouse for its flight crews. Oldfield was only lost to fire in the 1990s, with the exterior shell remaining.

Gustave Reinberg was the superintendent of American Forcite Powder Company (later known as Atlas Powder Company), located in what is today Shore Hills in Roxbury. The plant operated at the Lake from 1883 to 1932 manufacturing explosives and acids. This 1910 photograph shows Oldfield's grandeur.

This *c.* 1903 photograph of Byram Cove shows two of the three Sister Islands, as yet unbuilt. This would change in 1905 when Joseph R. King decided this was the perfect location for a cottage.

King connected two of the three islands and built a cottage, a boathouse complete with kitchen and dining room, and an icehouse. In 1912, King sold to Thomas Henderson. Henderson, the owner of Angler's Retreat, a rooming house on Cow Tongue Point, converted the property into the Sister Islands Hotel.

Carl Sherman, a former Attorney General of the State of New York, bought Sister Islands in the 1940s and converted the icehouse into a second home. It was during this time that a bridge was added, linking the islands with the mainland. Recent attempts to have a similar bridge built were denied by governing officials.

In 1894, Rev. Dr. Vincent Pisek, a Bohemian minister from New York City, purchased 4 acres of land in remote Byram Cove. After camping on the property for a season, the Pisek family built a large stone cottage. In a period before governmental control, Dr. Pisek took delight in dredging the lakefront around his house into an area of little canals which were dubbed "Little Venice" or "The Isles." Although Pisek's house is gone, the canals survive as Air Castle Isles.

31

Prior to electric refrigeration, ice was used to preserve food. From the mid-1800s to the 1930s, ice was a huge industry on Lake Hopatcong. At its peak, the Lake supported five major icehouses, employing hundreds of laborers during the ice-cutting season. As seen in this c. 1905 photograph, horses were widely used as they were considered more dependable than the machinery then available.

Ice was "harvested" and stored in icehouses until needed. A good season was considered to have occurred when the Lake could be harvested twice in one winter. Lake Hopatcong's ice was shipped by rail to such cities as Newark, Jersey City, and New York City. In this c. 1910 photograph, horses relax in front of the Sans Souci property off Elba Point.

Unlike Jefferson and Roxbury, Hopatcong had no major icehouses. However, there was a smaller icehouse in River Styx. This *c.* 1915 photograph shows Jack Sohner's icehouse just to the right of the Pagoda and West Side Church.

Prior to 1920, the easiest way to transport supplies around the Lake was by water. This 1910 photograph shows an ice delivery on its way.

From the building of the first cottages north of River Styx, it was concluded that a bridge was needed across Lake Hopatcong to access Landing by road. The first bridge, seen in this c. 1905 photograph, was constructed entirely of wood. It was erected in the 1880s at private expense. A steel bridge replaced it in 1909.

Prior to its development in the 1930s, Bear Pond was a favorite spot for a day's excursion or picnic. Many a summer visitor to Lake Hopatcong spent a day trying to find this delightful oasis on the trail from Byram Cove. This c. 1910 photograph shows a serene and undeveloped Bear Pond.

Three
Gem of the Jersey Hills

Visitors found that New Jersey's largest lake was easy to reach, had beautiful scenery, and its location—over 900 feet above sea level—meant lower daytime temperatures and cool evenings. Advertised as the "Jewel of the Mountains," Lake Hopatcong was a welcome respite from the hot summers of the urban centers to the east. As the railroads spurred tourism, hotels were quickly built to accommodate the visitors. Whereas prior to 1883 only four small hotels existed at the Lake, by 1900 over 40 hotels and rooming houses were operating along the booming shores of Lake Hopatcong, with over one-quarter of these being in the Borough of Hopatcong. There was a hotel for every taste and budget. From the 1880s to the 1930s, the Borough of Hopatcong became a major resort destination.

Since roads at the Lake were poor or nonexistent, the main source of transportation during Lake Hopatcong's early years was by water. As tourism developed, so did steamboat service. The Lake Hopatcong Steamboat Company, commonly known as the Black Line, was founded in 1886 and provided service from the railroads to all areas of the Lake. This photo finds the Black Line steamer *Mystic Shrine* in River Styx Cove, *c*. 1913.

The Hopatcong Steamboat Company, commonly known as the White Line, was founded *c*. 1890 as competition to the Black Line. When the White Line was unable to obtain the right to use the Morris Canal, it dredged the southernmost part of Lake Hopatcong, a then non-navigable, swampy area. This created Landing Channel, which the Hopatcong Steamboat Company used to bring its boats within a block of Landing Station. This *c*. 1905 photograph shows two White Line steamers at Sperry Springs dock.

36

Steamboats serviced all areas of the Lake. They had schedules with regular stops at the major hotels and other areas of importance. In addition, one could request steamboat pick-up by placing a flag on the dock. The largest—and only—double-decker steamboat on the Lake was the sidewheeler *Hopatcong*, part of the White Line, seen in this photograph taken around 1905.

For two decades, the Black Line and White Line had a very lively competition for business on Lake Hopatcong. But by the teens both were out of business, unable to effectively compete with bus and taxi service. After the demise of the White and Black Lines, smaller operations utilizing gas-powered boats continued to furnish water transportation around the Lake. By the end of the 1930s, they too lost out to motor vehicles.

BROOKLYN HOUSE

ONE MILE NORTH OF

LANDING, N. J.

ELMER ATNO, Propr.

OPEN ALL THE YEAR.

Summer and Transient Boarders taken.

CIGARS AND TOBACCO SOLD.

Prior to 1883, when regular railroad service to Lake Hopatcong began, Hopatcong had two small hotels—the Brooklyn House and the Hopatcong House. During Lake Hopatcong's peak tourist years, over a dozen hotels would operate in the Borough. The Brooklyn House opened in the 1870s.

Owned by the Atno family, whose descendants still reside in Hopatcong, the Brooklyn House was a small hotel located on what is now the corner of Lakeside Boulevard and Brooklyn-Stanhope Road. The hotel, seen here in a c. 1898 photograph, was completely destroyed by fire during the winter of 1900–1901.

Built just after the turn of the century, the Shady Lawn House was located just north of Hopatcong State Park, where West Shore Avenue now runs. The hotel could accommodate 30 guests. It was renamed the West Shore Hotel in 1914 and changed back to the Shady Lawn in 1929. The hotel, seen in this 1915 photograph, was destroyed by fire in December 1933.

As seen in this c. 1905 photograph, the Mountain View House was a large hotel which stood at the top of the hill in Atno Heights, where Stone Avenue runs today. Built in the 1890s, it had 65 rooms and advertised the largest dance hall (barely visible behind the trees on the right) and orchestra at Lake Hopatcong. It is believed to have been the first hotel at Lake Hopatcong to offer kosher food, in the early 1920s. The end came for the hotel when it was severely damaged by fire in May 1934.

Constructed on Point Pleasant in 1910 at a cost of $25,000, Justamere Lodge was a smaller hotel, advertising 21 rooms. Built of Pennsylvania brown stone brick, the hotel operated into the 1960s. For many of its years, it advertised as catering to a Christian clientele. The hotel, seen here in 1911, survives today as a private residence.

Located next door to Justamere Lodge on Point Pleasant, the Sussex House operated as a small hotel from the 1890s until the 1930s, advertising 16 rooms. Looking much the same today as in this *c.* 1910 photograph, the Sussex House survives today as a private residence.

Built in the 1880s by C.O. Brown and named Bella Vista, because of its spectacular view up the Lake, this cottage was later renamed Hillcrest by the Tolson family. It became a small hotel in the early 1930s, featuring dining and banquet facilities.

After only a few years, the Hillcrest Inn and Club was converted back to a private residence prior to World War II. In 1951, it was purchased as a clubhouse for the newly formed Garden State Yacht Club. It would serve this role until destroyed by fire in December 1984.

Hillcrest Inn and Club

Beautifully and Centrally Located on West Shore with seven mile view of the Lake

A La Carte Service at all hours. Catering to Banquets & Outings Private Sandy Bathing Beach. Apply for rates.

MUSIC

Telephone Hopatcong 86.   P. O. Box 192, Landing, N. J.

OPEN ALL YEAR
EUROPEAN AND AMERICAN PLAN

HOPATCONG HOUSE.

LAKE HOPATCONG ✒ ✒ ✒

MRS. FREDERICK MAST.

BEST ACCOMMODATIONS FOR SUMMER BOARDERS AND TRAVELERS.

—— OPEN ALL THE YEAR. ——

Post office: Landing, Morris Co., New Jersey.

The house is on the West side of the Lake, two miles from Hopatcong Station. The situation is extremely pleasant and the house is homelike and comfortable.
Heated rooms for cool weather.

GOOD FISHING AND GUNNING.   GOOD BOATS TO HIRE.

LIVERY IN CONNECTION. Conveyances of all descriptions.

Our wagons meet all important trains during the summer months, and will meet any train
at any time if notified by mail the day previous.

Believed to have been a tavern as early as the 1840s, the Hopatcong House was Lake Hopatcong's earliest hotel. Owned by Col. Joseph Sharp (for whom Sharp's Rock is named), it was reportedly used in its early years by fishermen and workers engaged in the timber and charcoal industries.

The Hopatcong House was owned by the Mast family for many years and was the site of the first meeting of the mayor and council for the Borough of Brooklyn on May 9, 1898. An early Lakeside Boulevard is visible to the right of the hotel in this 1911 photograph.

42

As the Hopatcong House property originally ran down to the Lake's shore, it maintained bathhouses, a dock, and a small pavilion. This 1911 photograph shows the original Hopatcong House property as well as two boathouses which still survive—the boathouse from Bird's Nest can be seen on the right and the boathouse/icehouse for the Reinberg estate on the left.

In 1966, the Hopatcong House finally succumbed to fire, as did most of the hotels built after it at the Lake. Most of the Hopatcong House property, such as the dock area seen in this c. 1905 photograph, now contains private residences. The Boulevard Pub stands on the actual hotel site. The livery, later the garage, had been sold in the early 1960s and transformed into the Villa Nova Hotel and Restaurant. It was later converted into apartments, and remains as such to this date.

43

The Forest Club was started by a group of businessmen who came to the Lake in the 1880s with their families. It consisted of a main hall surrounded by small cottages almost directly across from the Lake Hopatcong Yacht Club. In the early 1900s, the Forest was converted into a hotel. In the 1920s, it became Peter's Cottages and eventually was subdivided. Several of the original cottages survive today as private residences. In this c. 1910 photograph, the main hall and several of the cottages are visible.

Built in 1893 on Sharp's Rock, the Laurel House consisted of approximately 30 rooms. Hudson Maxim became the hotel's neighbor in 1904 when he built on adjoining land. His observatory can be seen to the left in this 1908 photograph. Maxim reportedly did not care for the manner in which the hotel was being managed (it was rumored that he did not care for the ragtime music being played there), so he purchased it in 1908.

Maxim renamed the establishment the Hotel Durban (his wife's maiden name) and leased the hotel to proprietors who would operate it to his liking. As seen in this c. 1915 photograph, the Durban featured a restaurant and grill which was open until midnight during the season. The hotel operated until 1929, when there were plans to convert it into a select family club, to be called the Maxim Club. Evidently the Depression prevented these plans from ever being implemented.

The hotel would burn in the years which followed, and in the early 1940s, James Francomacaro (chauffeur of Hudson Maxim and a Hopatcong councilman for many years) would build a private home on the site. The original stone walls, seen in this c. 1910 photograph, still surround the Francomacaro home on Sharp's Rock Road, but over the years the property was subdivided and it is no longer a lakefront property.

Unlike other hotels at Lake Hopatcong, the Colonial Inn was built to be fireproof. Located on the south side of River Styx Cove (currently 369 Lakeside Boulevard), this hotel, with some 40 rooms, was built of cement. Seen in this photograph, it opened for business in July 1911. Before the property could ever be fully landscaped, the hotel was destroyed by a gas explosion in August 1912. Being underinsured, it was not rebuilt.

Located on the south shore of River Styx Cove (currently 411 Lakeside Boulevard), The Greencroft was constructed as a one-story structure around 1911. After expanding several times, including the addition of the two upper floors in 1916 and the purchase of several surrounding cottages, the Greencroft advertised 45 rooms. Seen here c. 1940, it operated as a hotel into the 1960s and survives today as a private residence.

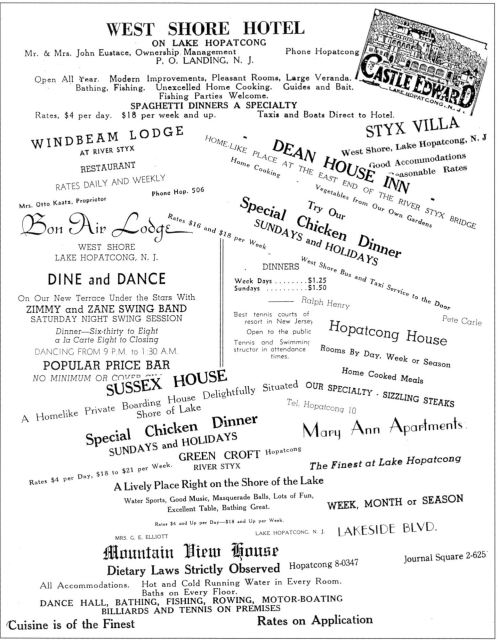
The hotel era at Lake Hopatcong was at its height from the 1880s to the 1930s. Its decline started in 1929 with the onset of the Depression. Many hotels and businesses succumbed as the nation's economic troubles wore on through the 1930s. As World War II consumed America, so it consumed Lake Hopatcong. Past frivolity largely disappeared as the Lake joined the war effort. Rationing of various materials and supplies made operating hotels difficult. In addition, gasoline rationing curtailed automobile traffic, which had become an increasingly significant portion of the Lake's business in the years before the war. Following the war, people began to head for newer and more exotic vacation areas, including the Catskills and Poconos, rather than the old standbys like Lake Hopatcong.

Camp Edward, Lake Hopatcong, N.J.

The grandest hotel in the Borough was undoubtedly Castle Edward. John P. Muller and his family first established a campsite at the Lake near Bertrand Island in the 1890s. Around the turn of the century Muller acquired property on the south shore of River Styx and established Camp Edward, named after his son. The campsite featured a boathouse, seen in this *c.* 1904 photograph.

In 1905, Muller built a one-level structure with some 20 rooms in the style of a 17th-century castle. A small island (sometimes referred to as Mush Island) was constructed in front of the hotel.

48

Within a few years, Muller added a second level to the back of the hotel, increasing its size to about 40 rooms. As seen in this 1912 photograph, the little island was converted to a gazebo-type structure with a curved concrete bridge from the mainland.

In 1913, Muller doubled the size of the hotel to 80 rooms by adding a third level, giving the structure a true castle-like appearance. As seen in this *c.* 1915 photograph, Castle Edward dominated River Styx for the next two decades.

Castle Edward featured an orchestra and ballroom, bowling alleys, billiards, and a sandy beach—all beginning at $12 per week! In 1917, a grill room and barber shop were added.

Mush Island was a favorite spot for guests and soon became the perfect spot for a photograph. This 1915 photograph shows Mush Island's final evolution, surrounded by the same concrete balustrade used elsewhere on the hotel site.

John P. Muller remained the owner of Castle Edward until his death in 1923. The hotel opened for the 1924 season under the management of Gilbert Muller, but quickly ran into trouble and was sold at auction in November 1924. Castle Edward was purchased by Frank Brindle of Paterson, who performed extensive renovations for the 1925 season.

Brindle operated the hotel until the Depression, when it was forced to close. During the winter of 1931 a fire struck the closed hotel, totally destroying the building. The land laid vacant, strewn with rubble for many years. Not until after World War II was the site redeveloped. The ornate walkways and roadside balustrade survived and can still be seen today at 429 Lakeside Boulevard.

The Castle Edward property was subdivided. The bulk of the property was used for Mary Ann's, a motel-like structure which incorporated the original grand exterior staircase and some of the beautiful stone walls. Mary Ann's was eventually sold to a group of families in a "cooperative" arrangement. Over the years, many of the original owners died and the property fell into disrepair. Under a new owner, there has been work to remodel the structure within the past year.

Opening in River Styx Cove around 1905, Styx Villa (seen in this *c*. 1914 photograph) was enlarged in 1911 to include some 25 rooms. In the 1940s it would be known as Camp Everett and then as the Grand View Hotel. In the mid-1950s, this hotel became the home of the Lake Hopatcong Jewish Community Center. After the Center constructed a new building in 1972, on the adjoining property of the old Brief's Bungalow Colony, the building fell into disrepair and was finally demolished around 1990.

In 1914, D.B. Smith's impressive cottage Westerly (seen here *c.* 1910) was converted into the Hotel Bon Air and Cottages. It was comprised of the main building and ten cottages, with a boathouse added in 1915. In 1925, the main building was greatly expanded and modified, creating some 33 rooms. Following the renovation, the hotel was renamed Bon Air Lodge.

Under the subsequent ownership of the Tolson family, who operated the Bristol Hotel in New York City, and the Shustin family, Bon Air Lodge (seen here around 1955) remained vibrant even as other Lake Hopatcong hotels closed. Utilizing its 10 acres, four tennis courts, and a sense for what the public wanted, the Bon Air remained popular through the 1950s. It was sold by the Shustin's in 1960 and became the Arrowcrest Lodge. In 1970 it was destroyed by fire and the current Arrowcrest was built on the site.

One of the Borough's oldest hotels, the Ithanell started as a boathouse with two cottages in the 1880s. Shortly thereafter a large house was erected and an even larger annex was added in 1897, giving the hotel some 35 rooms. The original boathouse and an undeveloped River Styx are seen in this 1911 photograph.

The name Ithanell supposedly came from the men who built the first two cottages on the property. They came from Ithaca, New York, and the name is a combination of Ithaca and the neighboring college, Cornell. The owner liked the name and kept it is as the name for the hotel. This 1911 photograph shows the main building.

The Ithanell operated until World War II. Following the war, the main buildings were removed and the site was subdivided. One of the original cottages survives today, having been enlarged over the ensuing years. The name is preserved by the road on which the hotel was located. The hotel occupied what is today 60–68 Ithanell Road.

Opened in 1894, Angler's Retreat (also known as Henderson's Hotel) was located on Cow Tongue Point. In this c. 1905 photograph, a steamboat is seen leaving the hotel, which catered to fisherman. Hudson Maxim acquired the hotel and donated a perpetual lease in the land to the Maxim Park Yacht Club, which utilized the site from 1915 through the late 1920s. The hotel was greatly renovated to serve as a clubhouse for the yacht club and survives today as a lovely private residence.

Corinthian Lodge, seen in this *c.* 1915 photograph, was one of Hopatcong's smallest hotels, opening around 1912. With only about 10 rooms and a few bungalows, it was located between the River Styx Bridge and what is now Lighthouse Marina. In 1937 it was renovated and became Windbeam Lodge. In the 1940s, it became Glen Cove Lodge and operated into the 1950s. It later served as home for Bridge Marine and was torn down in the mid-1990s.

In addition to the hotels, many rooming houses operated over the years in the Borough of Hopatcong. Places such as Mrs. Kaatz's, Deane House, Inverness, Kelly's Hilltop, Lakeside, Hillside Cottage, Birchwood Terrace, Neko Lodge, Yates Villa, Bergmann House, and the Castle Atno all opened their doors to the tourist trade during Lake Hopatcong's great hotel era. This photo shows the Deane House Inn, *c.* 1940, located near the River Styx Bridge on Deane Road.

Four

Stargazing in Hopatcong

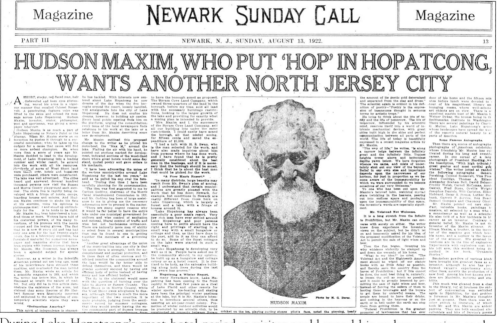

During Lake Hopatcong's great hotel period, a visitor could spend his or her vacation at the Lake and enjoy non-stop activities and entertainment. On a typical summer evening the choice of activities might include listening to jazz at various hotels, dancing at one of the dance halls, entertainment by big-name Vaudeville stars at one of the pavilions, a dock or theme party, or a visit to one of the Lake's two amusement parks. Weekends were filled with events—from boat races to water carnivals, to beauty pageants, to recovering from the previous evening's activities—there were few dull moments. It was during this period that the Lake, and particularly Hopatcong, became a destination for the rich and famous.

Referred to by Thomas Edison as "the most versatile man in America," Hudson Maxim was an inventor, scientist, author, and explosives expert. First drawn to Lake Hopatcong while working with American Forcite Powder Company at the turn of the century, he bought 600 acres on the west shore in 1901. In 1904, Maxim built his main house, initially known as Maximhurst and then simply as Maxim Park. Maxim's greatest fame came from his inventions in modern warfare, as the inventor of smokeless powder and other propellants, shells, and torpedoes. Ironically, he often lectured and wrote on the need for arbitration and not war. He spoke and wrote prolifically on other topics as well—from his opposition of maintaining the Morris Canal, to his disdain of Prohibition, to his love of poetry and boxing. He was a confidant of presidents, having spent time with at least three. While he maintained a townhouse in Brooklyn, New York, Maxim spent most of the year at Maxim Park when not traveling. This 1910 photograph shows most of the main buildings of Maxim Park. The two houses on the left were used for guests, tennis courts and laboratory were on top of the hill, and the large building in the middle of the hill was his main residence. At the shoreline was the boathouse and to the right his observatory/icehouse. The large building seen on the right of the photograph is the Durban Hotel.

Although he had a chauffeur, Maxim was a car enthusiast and loved to drive. Having lost one hand as a result of a laboratory accident, his enthusiasm for fast driving became a local legend. Passionate about the Lake, Maxim also saw the opportunities in its development. In 1910, he purchased the Byram Cove Land Company, which consisted of over 650 acres and 2.5 miles of lakefront. He now owned approximately three-quarters of the existing Borough of Hopatcong.

With two guest houses and a large main house, the Maxim's regularly entertained guests from all walks of life. Many a dignitary spent time at Maxim Park as witnessed by the July Fourth weekend in 1910, when visitors included Francis DuPont, Rex Beach, and Annie Oakley, among others. Some, such as great American poet Edwin Markham, would stay for weeks. This c. 1925 photograph captures a group of visitors at Maxim Park. Maxim, with his wife, Lillian, is third from the right in the second row.

In 1906, Maxim built his famous Venetian-style boathouse, which would dominate the west shore for the next 50 years. Built of stone and wood with two steel girders, it projected out over the water and resembled a medieval fortress. It had three floors and stone fireplaces. This 1909 photograph captures the beauty of the boathouse.

This photograph shows Maxim and longtime friend Thomas Edison in the 1920s. Maxim died May 6, 1927, at Maxim Park. In 1929, a monument in his honor was erected at Hopatcong State Park. While his main house and boathouse were regrettably torn down in the late 1950s, several other Maxim Park buildings survive today. The two guest houses and the garage are private residences, and the unique round icehouse/observatory has been converted to a rathskeller.

During the great hotel period, the Lake became a popular destination for Vaudeville and Burlesque stars, who generally had time off in the summer when many theaters closed. While some preferred and could afford hotels, many chose to rent or buy small houses in the Northwood section of Hopatcong, which became known as the "actor's colony." No entertainer had a greater impact on Hopatcong than Joe Cook.

Sometimes billed as "one-man Vaudeville," Joe Cook was adept at juggling, telling jokes, acting, singing, dancing, and mime. Cook was known for his good-natured comedy and infectious smile. By the 1920s, he was a headliner on the Vaudeville circuit. In this photo, Joe and his family are seen at Pine Tree Point, spending their first summer at Lake Hopatcong in 1924.

While renting at the Lake in 1924, the Cook's purchased the Boulders cottage in Davis Cove. After extensive renovations, Cook renamed it Sleepless Hollow, an appropriate name considering the many parties and festivities which would be held there. In typical Cook style, many gags were built into the house as part of the renovation. Just about anyone who was anyone during the 1920s and 1930s visited Sleepless Hollow. Joe is seen here with one of the gnomes which were a theme used throughout the house.

Graduating from Vaudeville, Joe Cook became a Broadway musical comedy star, performing in such hits as *Rain or Shine*, *Fine and Dandy*, and *Hold Your Horses*. Cook, never a fan of Hollywood, only made two full-length features—*Rain or Shine*, directed by Frank Capra in 1930, and *Arizona Mahoney* in 1936. Joe loved boating on the Lake. Joe is seen entering his boathouse in his beloved Belle Isle Bearcat speedboat *Four Hawaiians*, named after his most famous skit.

The 26 acres of Sleepless Hollow gave Cook room to build a nine-hole golf course in 1925. Not surprisingly, a few gags were built in. The tee for the first hole was on top of a water tower, and the green for the ninth hole was built so that any ball landing on it rolled into the hole. During the 1930s, Cook was popular on radio, hosting two variety series and regularly appearing as a guest on others.

The reflections of Joe Cook and Babe Ruth are seen while golfing at Sleepless Hollow in 1939. Cook's career was shortened when diagnosed with Parkinson's disease in 1940 at age 50. His Hopatcong house was sold in 1941, ending a very successful 17-year run. While the golf course is long-gone and now covered with houses, Sleepless Hollow survives today and has just been remodeled. Despite being one of the biggest stars of his day, Joe Cook is sadly unknown to many today, having performed in an era before television and having made few films.

Joe Cook regularly mentioned Lake Hopatcong in his acts and on radio. His Hopatcong home was regularly featured in magazines and newspaper articles of the 1920s and 1930s. Cook truly was Lake Hopatcong's ambassador to the world.

Owen McGiveney was a popular Vaudevillian, making his mark as a "quick change artist." Known for the speed of his changes and the ability to quickly transform himself with make-up, he would play as many as five roles in a 10-minute act. In later years, McGiveney became a character actor, appearing in such films as *Showboat*, *Brigadoon*, and *My Fair Lady*.

From 1919 to 1945, McGiveney and his family spent most summers at their cottage, Owendale, in the Lookout Mountain section of River Styx. In this *c.* 1930 photograph, we see McGiveney, at left, in his prized *Gibson Girl*.

P.J. Monahan, seen here with his wife at Pine Tree Point, was one of America's leading illustrators during the first part of this century. His work graced many magazines and books. He summered at Pine Tree Point from the late teens until his death in 1931.

This 1912 cover of *Leslie's* features Monahan's work. He also did numerous covers for *Munsey, Judge, Ladies Home Journal, Pearson's,* and *Cosmopolitan.* He was the favorite illustrator for famed author Edward Rice Burroughs. Monahan's son Joseph still resides at Lake Hopatcong.

Miss Vinnie Phillips was a dancer and actress who became synonymous with the role of Sister Betty in the play *Tobacco Road*, which she portrayed in more than 3,000 performances. She visited Northwood for the first time in the 1920s, then bought a cottage which she owned until her death in 1977. She is seen with her children at the Lake in this *c. 1920s* photograph.

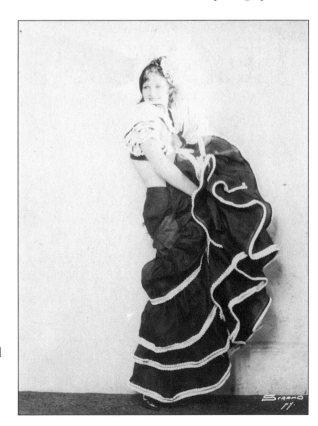

Vinnie Phillips' daughter Buster was also an entertainer in Vaudeville and Burlesque. She lived in Northwood from 1946 until her death in 1996, under her married name of Sanchez. Here she is at the peak of her career in the 1930s.

Jeanette MacDonald was among Hollywood's top stars of the 1930s, appearing in such movies as *The Merry Widow* and *Naughty Marietta* with leading men like Maurice Chevalier, Clark Gable, and, of course, Nelson Eddy. During the mid-1920s, while working on Broadway, she dated a member of the Ohmeis family, who owned the Hopatcong cottage known as Moorings.

Moorings, a large cottage located between Sharp's Rock and Pickerel Point, was originally built by the Moore family, hence its name. The house, more recently known as Pearly Gates, does not look much different today than it does in this *c.* 1915 photograph.

Bert Lahr was a leading comedian in Burlesque and Vaudeville, who became a major musical comedy star on Broadway from the late 1920s through the 1960s. He appeared in many films but will always be remembered as the beloved Cowardly Lion in *The Wizard of Oz*. Lahr spent significant vacation time at Lake Hopatcong, first renting in Northwood from 1918 into the 1920s, and later staying at Lake hotels. He is seen third from left in Northwood, *c.* 1922.

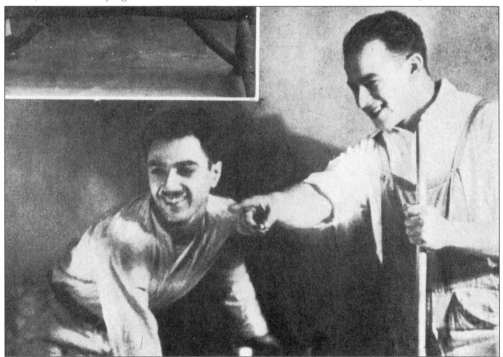

William and Joe Mandel were famous Vaudeville acrobats and comedians. They were neighbors of Owen McGiveney in the Lookout Mountain section of River Styx during the 1920s and 1930s.

Bud Abbott, the famous straight man of the Abbott and Costello comedy team, summered with his family at Northwood during the mid-and late-1930s, just prior to teaming with Lou Costello. During this period, Bud was performing in Vaudeville with his wife, Betty, and other performers. His son, Bud Jr., was a featured performer in the Northwood Kiddie Reviews of 1935 and 1936.

Arthur (Billy) Green was a Vaudevillian who started as a pianist, playing for the famous dance team of Vernon and Castle, among others. He also appeared with his wife as the song team of Green and Lafell. His greatest fame came as a composer, writing many hits of the day. The Greens first came to Northwood and their cottage, Billie Hut, in the 1920s. After retiring, they lived here full time until his death in 1957.

The longtime owner of the New York Giants baseball team, Horace Stoneham, first came to Lake Hopatcong while dating his future wife in the early 1920s. Mr. and Mrs. Stoneham then purchased a house in Northwood and summered there with their children through the early 1950s. Local youngsters were thrilled by the sighting of players visiting Mr. Stoneham on off days. This 1924 photograph shows a young Horace Stoneham on the right.

Cornelia "Corky" Gilissen, a native of Elmhurst, Queens, had been swimming at her parents summer cottage in Northwood for 15 years when she qualified for the U.S. Olympic team as a platform diver in 1936. She finished fifth in her event and was welcomed back to the Lake as a champion. Following the Olympics, Corky and her sister Jo, an accomplished swimmer, went on national tour with the 1937 *Water Follies*.

This former resident of Stone Avenue thrilled Hopatcong when she won the Miss New Jersey pageant in 1963. At the Miss America pageant, Janet Adams won the talent competition. After a career as an actress, she is now a minister and lives in California.

Hopatcong's glory as a resort is captured in this photograph of Mardi Gras in 1926, held as part of that year's Lake Hopatcong Carnival. In the middle of the photo is Hudson Maxim, who was "Father of the Lake." To Maxim's right is Joe Cook, voted King of the Carnival, and to the left is Estelle Glasser (daughter of William Glasser and a successful performer), who was Queen. Surrounding the "royal party" is their "court," complete with jesters.

Five

Location is Everything

As Lake Hopatcong's popularity grew, people naturally became interested in owning property. Real estate developers began to open up large stretches of property around the Lake and the development boom was on.

Developing tracts of land at and around Lake Hopatcong began in the late 19th century and grew in the years prior to World War I. Spurred by the economic boom of the 1920s, development accelerated. Though slowed by the Depression, development still continued and accelerated again following World War II. Here is a typical cottage built by the Orben family, early Hopatcong developers.

Growth was spurred by a lack of zoning regulations, and since building was exclusively intended for summer use, privacy from one's neighbors was unimportant. As a result, little room was left between structures in many developments, as seen in this *c.* 1930 photograph.

The Byram Cove Land Company was the earliest large developer at the Lake, being very active during the 1890s and the turn of the century. In 1910, the company and its 650 acres were bought out by Hudson Maxim.

The Hopatcong Park Land Company developed much of the land between Lake Hopatcong and Bear Pond in the 1920s. It is safe to say that it's been a while since lakefront property was sold for $10 per foot.

Public Dock, Byram Cove, Lake Hopatcong,
at Hopatcong Park Estates.

Since the development companies were also selling non-lakefront properties, it was common practice to preserve land for a public dock and swimming area so that everyone had access to the Lake. This 1920s photograph shows the public or community dock built in Byram Cove by the Hopatcong Park Land Company for its Hopatcong Park Estates development.

North End View of Bear Pond
at Hopatcong Park Estates.

At 1.5 miles long and .75 miles wide, Bear Pond was a favorite spot for a day's excursion or picnic in Hopatcong's early years. Hopatcong Park Estates development reached Bear Pond by 1930, and despite the country's financial woes, much development occurred there during the 1930s.

Following Mary Ingram's death, the extensive Ingram family homestead was sold, and in 1925 the development of Lake Hopatcong Gardens began on the property. This development consisted of most of Ingram Cove as well as a portion of the land between Point Pleasant and Hopatcong State Park.

George W. Campbell founded the Lake Hopatcong Steamboat Company and was responsible for much early development at the Lake. His leadership of the West Side Association helped spur growth on the west shore. Following his death in 1923, his son continued the business, as witnessed by this 1925 advertisement.

78

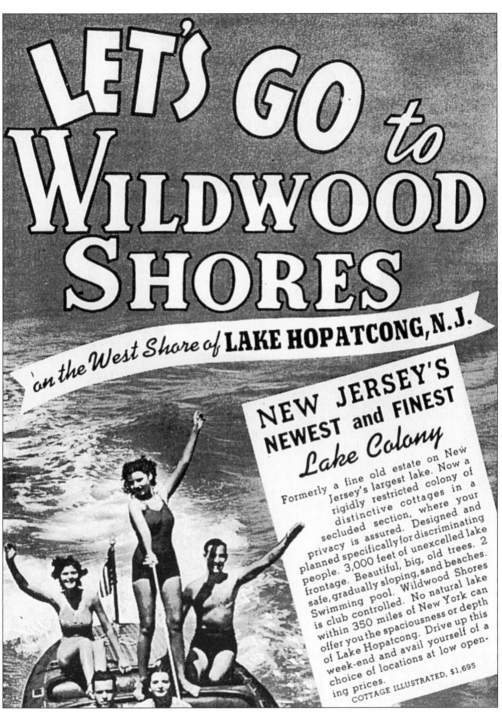

LET'S GO to WILDWOOD SHORES

on the West Shore of LAKE HOPATCONG, N.J.

NEW JERSEY'S NEWEST and FINEST Lake Colony

Formerly a fine old estate on New Jersey's largest lake. Now a rigidly restricted colony of distinctive cottages in a secluded section, where your privacy is assured. Designed and planned specifically for discriminating people. 3,000 feet of unexcelled lake frontage. Beautiful, big, old trees. 2 safe, gradually sloping, sand beaches. Swimming pool. Wildwood Shores is club controlled. No natural lake within 350 miles of New York can offer you the spaciousness or depth of Lake Hopatcong. Drive up this week-end and avail yourself of a choice of locations at low opening prices. COTTAGE ILLUSTRATED, $1,695

R.L. Edwards' Wildwood property began to be developed in 1934. Advertising 60 acres and 3,000 feet of lake frontage, it appealed to "discriminating people" in a "rigidly restricted colony." Such thinly veiled discriminatory statements were not uncommon during this era— only certain groups were welcome to purchase. This classic advertisement dates from 1940.

The concept of "restricted" developments was not limited to Wildwood Shores. As early as 1925, Lake Hopatcong Shores was "catering to the better class buyer" and assuring a "restricted colony." Unfortunately, in this respect, Hopatcong was just a sign of its times.

The original development of the Hopatcong Hills was actually in conjunction with a subscription plan sponsored by the *Newark Ledger* in 1931. Selling points for this development were the bathing beach being built at Hudson Avenue and the clubhouse, both for the use of Hopatcong Hills residents. The Hopatcong Hills Beach survives, but the original log cabin clubhouse burned in 1948. During the late 1940s and 1950s, the "Hills" would be developed in a more conventional manner.

COTTAGES NEAR PAGODA, RIVER STYXS, LAKE HOPATCONG, N.J.

The practice of renting a piece of land on which to pitch a tent, a popular way to vacation in the Borough's early years, was gradually replaced by the bungalow colony vacation. Visitors could rent basic cottages and, for an additional fee, such items as blankets, pots, and pans. Bungalow colonies sprouted up around the Lake in the teens and 1920s and continued into the 1960s. River Styx was a favorite spot for bungalow colonies, as seen in this *c.* 1940 photograph. Some of these bungalows now form the Pagoda Condominium.

GREGSON'S COTTAGES

FOR RENT—Completely Furnished

ON THE WEST SHORE   P. O. BOX 17, HOPATCONG, N. J.

2 and 4 Rooms $150 to $325 a Season

5 Rooms, Lake Front, $400 to $500 a Season

Running Water, Electric Lights, Indoor Toilets

Big, Sandy Beach.   Six Minutes from D. L. & W. Station

West Shore Bus and Taxi Service Direct to Cottages

One of River Styx's largest bungalow colonies was Gregson's Cottages (seen in this 1925 advertisement), which was located on the property where the Lake Hopatcong Jewish Community Center now stands. During the 1950s and 1960s it was known as Brief's Bungalow Colony. A few of the original cottages still survive on the property.

In the Crescent Cove section of River Styx was Lookout Mountain Village. Offering water and toilets in each cottage, it must be considered an upscale bungalow colony, as such amenities were not common at the Lake in the 1920s.

This 1930s photograph shows classic Hopatcong cottages on Byram Cove. With the construction of Route 80 in the 1960s, Hopatcong started to become a largely year-round community. Structures such as this, which may have sold for a few thousand dollars in the 1950s, began to be converted and enlarged. Many a Hopatcong resident lives in such a converted cottage today.

83

No community can develop without schools, fire departments, police departments, and houses of worship. The Borough of Brooklyn's first school was a structure inherited from Byram and located on Brooklyn-Stanhope Road, close to what is now Hopatcong State Park. Known as Brooklyn School, it was a true one-room wooden schoolhouse, encompassing eight grades. This 1898 photograph shows the school's 15 students in front of the school.

In 1908, a new one-room stone schoolhouse, known as Hopatcong School, was constructed on the old Sanford farm in River Styx, where the orchard was formerly located. The school is seen here shortly after completion. In 1925, two additional rooms were added to the structure.

The student body had grown by the time this 1925 photograph was taken. Hopatcong School was renamed the Hudson Maxim School shortly after Maxim's death in 1927.

PUBLIC SCHOOL, HOPATCONG, N.J.

Additional rooms were added to the Hudson Maxim School in 1949 and 1951. Further renovations and an enlargement in 1955 resulted in the original portion of the school being demolished. As Hopatcong has grown, so has the school, evolving into the Hudson Maxim School of today—over 20 classrooms serving just two grades!

The Hopatcong Volunteer Fire Department was organized in 1923. Fred Modick was the chief of the department when this photograph was taken in 1929. Modick would become mayor in 1936, upon the death of Perley Boomer, and serve in this capacity for the next 30 years—by far the longest period of any mayor in Hopatcong's history.

The original volunteer force, known as Company No. 1, would dissolve as additional fire companies were organized to serve the entire Borough. This was particularly essential as there was no paved road connecting River Styx to Northwood until 1936. Northwood's Company No. 2 is the oldest of the three Hopatcong fire companies.

Charles Thompson, owner of Northwood Boat Works, first fitted a pump to a small boat for the Borough's use in 1925. In 1948, Thompson purchased a 36-foot-long surplus Navy boat which had served as a communications boat during the D-Day invasion of Normandy. A councilman and fire commissioner, Thompson spent much of his spare time equipping the boat, the *Perley Boomer* (shown above), and it became part of Company No. 2 in 1949. It sank in 1959, and was eventually replaced by a new fireboat appropriately named the *Charles Thompson*.

This 1932 photograph shows the Hopatcong Police Force, consisting of three patrolmen, two special officers, the police commissioner, and the chief of police. The chief received $1,000 per year while the patrolmen were paid 65¢ per hour. The department had one vehicle, a 1929 Ford touring car. The communications system consisted of a series of red beacon lights throughout the Borough which could be activated when there was a need to notify the force.

Rev. Dr. Gessler had held services on his property, Tangle Wild, during the latter 19th and early 20th centuries. After the Hopatcong School was built in River Styx in 1908, services were transferred to this one-room school. In 1911, residents built the Borough's first church. As seen in this photograph, the cornerstone for the West Side Church was laid on July 2, 1911. The church was non-denominational, and Gessler preached there until his death in 1925.

In 1949, the church became the West Side Methodist Church (now the West Side United Methodist Church) after a vote of the congregation. Struck by fire in 1968, the inside of the church was gutted. The congregation built a new church in 1971 on Maxim Drive. The original church building, walls still solid, was incorporated into the Pagoda structure to form a large building originally known as Len E's Pagoda and for many years as the Lighthouse Disco.

ST. JOSEPH'S R.C. CHURCH,
LAKE HOPATCONG, N.J.

Hopatcong had two St. Joseph's Roman Catholic Churches, one in River Styx (seen in this *c.* 1940 photograph) and one in Northwood. Built in 1924, where Maxim School's playground is now located, the River Styx church collapsed from snow in 1948. Services moved around River Styx for the next 10 years until St. Jude's was built on Maxim Drive in 1958. St. Joseph's original staircase is still visible today on Lakeside Boulevard.

ST. JOSEPH'S R.C. CHURCH
NORTHWOOD, LAKE HOPATCONG, N.J.

Catholic services began in Northwood at Glasser's Pavilion in 1928. St. Joseph's of Northwood was built in 1930. The church, seen in this *c.* 1940 photograph, continued services into the late 1960s before its congregation moved to St. Jude's. The building survived until *c.* 1990 when it was torn down and replaced by a residence.

BYRAM BAY CHRISTIAN CHURCH

The Byram Bay Christian Church has already opened the season of 1931 and the Sunday School is in full swing; there is a need for at least two more teachers.

The regular Church services will begin next Sunday, July 5th, with Mr. Van Waanderen as the speaker.

Any one who has attended these services in past seasons will need no urging to come but if you have never attended come to the little church on the hillside just above Sperry Springs and enjoy the splendid singing and listen to the stirring message from Brother Van and then we know you will come again.

Sunday School meets at 10 A. M. Church service 11 A. M.

•• •• ••

The Byram Bay Christian Church, a non-denominational church located in Sperry Springs, was built on a lot donated by Hudson Maxim in 1925. The small quaint church remains vibrant and is Hopatcong's oldest active church.

The Lake Hopatcong Jewish Community Center was founded in the late 1940s and, as seen in this 1950 listing, conducted services in the Grand View Hotel (the old Styx Villa), before purchasing the building. The Jewish Center constructed its own building on adjoining land in 1972.

Six

The Place to Meet

PETERS'

**WEST SHORE GARAGE, BUS AND TAXI
SERVICE**

PHONE HOPATCONG 250   DAY AND NIGHT

Train Service	Garage Service
Bus and Taxis Meet All Trains	Peters' Garage is Located on Main West Shore Road Adjoining Hopatcong Post Office
Special Rates to Parties Seeking Hotel Accommodations, Furnished Bungalows, or Building Plots, upon presentation of this Booklet.	ALL GENERAL REPAIRS
Reduced Rates to Commuters	Gasoline, Oils, Grease, Michelin Tires and Tubes
Touring Cars for Hire by Hour, Trip or Day	A Phone Call will bring You a Service Car

GREEN BUS SERVICE
Between
SPERRY SPRINGS, RIVER STYX and LACKAWANNA R. R.

MEETS ALL TRAINS

For much of its history, the Borough of Hopatcong revolved around tourism and resort activities. This is reflected by many of the businesses and establishments which called Hopatcong home. Peters' Garage was located on Lakeside Boulevard on the old property of the Forest Hotel, along with a restaurant, general store, and post office. The post office moved to River Styx in 1934, the garage was torn down in 1936, the general store closed in 1941, and the property is now residential.

Early stores in Hopatcong were often bare bones, especially in the outer areas like Sperry Springs. This *c.* 1910 photograph shows the summer store at Camp Sperry.

Frantz's General Store and Post Office was located on Maxim Drive in Sperry Springs during the late 1930s. The store had gas pumps and much more. The Sperry Springs Post Office would move to a general store off the corner of Maxim Drive and Hudson Avenue. Sperry Springs maintained its own post office until 1966.

In the early years, when roads around Lake Hopatcong were poor or non-existent, most commerce was by water. For lakefront homeowners, dockside deliveries were common, as seen in this 1929 photograph.

During the teens, the store in Northwood was Harry Anderson's, located approximately where the Glasser Post Office is today.

As a vacation area, Bear Pond also had its share of restaurants and bars. Here is the Bear Pond Restaurant, c. 1940. Adolph's Beer Garden, located between Lake Hopatcong and Bear Pond, was another popular spot .

Located on the corner of Hopatchung Road and Chincopee Avenue, Anson's Store was the first real store in Hopatcong, opening c. 1905.

After a coat of stucco, Anson's Store
begins to look more familiar by the 1920s.

Anson's became Nan Pratt's, a Hopatcong favorite from the 1950s through the 1970s. Known for homemade pies and salads, lines were common on Saturdays and Sundays. In recent years, the location evolved from a grocery to a delicatessen, Jimmy O's, and now the Alps. The post office, next door in this 1960s photograph, would move to larger space up the street. A restaurant would move into the old post office for a short while, before the brick structure was removed.

One of the favorite establishments in Hopatcong's history was started by M. Kjellman aboard a houseboat around 1908. It was located in River Styx Cove, next to the bridge.

By 1912, the houseboat was gone and a snack bar/restaurant in the shape of a Japanese pagoda was erected. It must have been fun to enjoy a refreshment in this Japanese-inspired building while looking across at the awesome Castle Edward Hotel. This c. 1915 photograph shows the veranda around the Pagoda.

This *c.* 1915 photograph shows how the Pagoda was built to the water's edge. In the late 1920s, the Kjellman's sold it to the Osterbloom family, who would operate the Pagoda for the next 40 years. In addition to the lunch counter and soda fountain, gas pumps were added on the Lake for boats and on the road for cars. The Pagoda had bungalows and was a popular spot at which to rent boats and canoes.

In this *c.* 1940 photograph, the veranda has been enclosed and a small porch added. In the 1960s, an addition known as the Lobster Shack was added to the building, then Len E's Pagoda. The neighboring gutted church was then purchased and added on, creating an immense restaurant which proved too large to successfully operate. During the 1970s and 1980s, the building became one of New Jersey's most popular dance clubs as The Lighthouse. Since then, several businesses have struggled here.

POST OFFICE, BYRAM COVE, N.J. ON LAKE HOPATCONG

Located at the southern-most part of Byram Cove were the Byram Post Office and a tavern. The post office operated from the 1930s through the late 1950s.

The tavern was known as Jerry's and later as the Cove Bar for many years. The bar burned in the 1950s and was rebuilt. Later occupants at the site included the Four D's, Pappy's Roadhouse, and Cheers.

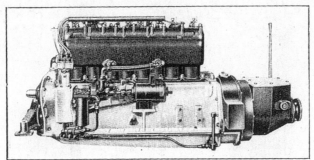
Northwood Boat and Engine Works opened in the mid-1920s. It would become very well known in the 1970s as Wayne's Marine, specializing in the restoration of antique boats under the careful attention of Wayne Mocksfield. After Wayne sold the business, it has once again become known as Northwood Boat Works, with John and Kim Kadimik preserving our wooden boat heritage.

In the summer of 1955, Hurricane Diane swamped the Northeast, as seen in this photograph of Northwood Boat Works.

A look back at 100 years of business. . . .

THE FAIRWAYS

Northern New Jersey's Foremost Recreation Center

WEST SHORE

Adjoining Lake Hopatcong Golf Club, N. J.

4 Bowling Alleys
4 Shuffleboards
Wines and Liquors

Anyone on the West Shore in Need of

- ICE -

Call "JACK"

The Dependable Ice Man   Telephone Hopatcong 265

JACK SOHNER, RIVER STYX

Tel. HOpatcong 8-0355

RIVER STYX GULF
Tires, Batteries etc. Ice Dock
GENERAL AUTO REPAIRS

P. E. BOOMER
CIVIL ENGINEER AND SURVEYOR
Edsall Road, Hopatcong, N. J.
Telephone Hop. 526

"LE BLEU'S"
WEST SHORE RESTAURANT
Opposite Maxim's School
STRICTLY HOME COOK...
River Styx

Dining and Dancing

HOPATCONG STORE AND POST OFFICE
Under New Management
On West Shore—Main Road from Landing
MOST MODERATE PRICED GROCER ON LAKE
Complete Line of Delicatessen
Staple and Fancy Groceries — CANDY — CIGARS
MOGLIA'S FRENCH ICE CREAM
Successor to Fred Peters
PETER RUNDLE, Prop.   Telephone: 53-J Ho.

MRS. OTTO KAATZ
TAVERN
AT SPERRY SPRINGS
BAR & GRILL   Meats — Groceries

Delicatessen

THE PAGODA
RIVER STYX
NEWSPAPERS — MAGAZINES
REFRESHMENTS
SAFE, SANDY BATHING BEACH
Ideal for Children
SPEED BOATS   ROW BOATS   CANOES

NOW IS YOUR CHANCE TO VISIT THE

MAD HOUSE

Our Amateur Shows are Famous
Our Two Bars Cooling
Our Food Delicious
And Our Orchestra Makes You Dance

Just for Fun!

WEST SHORE, HOPA...

Nan Pratt's COUNTRY STORE

MARTY'S
GENERAL STORE
DELICATESSEN - GROCERIES - ICE CREAM
FRESH FRUITS AND VEGETABLES
A BANNER STORE
Tel. Hopatcong 193
West Shore   LAKESIDE

RIVER STYX BRIDGE
THE PLACE TO EAT
THE PLACE TO MEET
THE PLACE TO MEET
UNDER NEW MANAGEMENT

How To Keep Cool

Hopatcong Theatre
RIVER STYX

Grand Opening Saturday
BIG DOUBLE FEATURES
Saturday and Sunday
"THE AGE OF DESIRE"
A First National Picture
"THE MAN FROM WYOMING"
A Universal Picture
Day Dreams and Buster Keaton Comedy

Tuesday, July 1st—
TOM MIX in
"EYES OF THE FOREST"
"The Huntsman," a Cook Comedy
Fox News

Wednesday, July 2nd—
"THE ... " TAYLOR
Novelty ..., " Comedy
Educ ...al Scenic—Runaway Day

VAN'S MARKET
PRIME MEATS
Groceries, Vegetables, Frosted Foods
RIVER STYX   Phone Hopatcong 142

..THE VENICE..
(Formerly River Styx Casino)
High - Class Italian Restaurant
West Shore, at the end of River Styx Bridge
REGULAR CHICKEN DINNER $1.50
Spaghetti Our Specialty
A La Carte Service at Moderate Prices
Telephone Hopatcong 60
AL SANCHIRICO, J. J. PERPETTO & BOB SANCHIRICO, Proprietors

Dancing

AT ANDY'S
ON-THE-STYX
Rowboats, Canoes, Motorboat
By Day, Week, or Hour
DANCING EVERY EVENING
Hopatcong, N. J.

GROGAN'S GARAGE
Specializing in Repairs on all makes of Cars
(First Garage North of Country Club)
Phone
JOHN or EDDIE
Day Service Hor
Nite Service H

KRANICH'S
"The Store of a Million Items"
SPORTING GOODS
...VARE   GENERAL MERCHANDISE
...Styx   Phone Hop. 566-W

Rose and Eddie's
BLUE GOOSE TAVERN
WEST SHORE, LAKE HOPATCONG, NEW JERSEY
COCKTAIL HOUR EVERY AFTERNOON FROM 1 'till 6
Where Courtesy is a Pleasure

MINIATURE GOLF
at the River Styx Bridge
Day & Evening — Cool & Shady
18 Hole Course

Announcing Opening of the Only Genuine

Chinese - American Restaurant
The New LOG CABIN Tea Garden
River Styx. Tel. Hop. 586. Coyle & Rynn, Props.
SPECIAL LUNCHEON, 50c   REGULAR DINNER, 75c
ALL KINDS OF CHINESE DISHES MADE UP TO TAKE OUT
Orchestra—Free Dancing—Beer on Draft.

Log Cabin Grill
Coolest Spot on the Lake
Famous Music Nightly. Entertainment.
No Cover Charge.

HOPATCONG GENERAL STORE
WEST SHORE   LAKESIDE BOULEVARD
DELICATESSEN — GROCERIES
FRESH FRUITS AND VEGETABLES
FOUNTAIN SERVICE
WAR & DELADE, Props.

... and 100 years of fun.

In 1918, a public dock was built at Northwood. Near the dock, William Glasser established a general store, pavilion, and icehouse in 1921. Glasser's, seen here shortly after it opened, became the local gathering place.

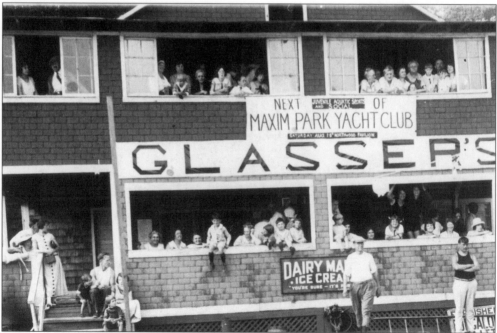

William Glasser treated his establishment as if it was the town meeting hall, making it readily available. Glasser's pavilion was frequently used for dances and other fund-raising activities. The neighboring Vaudeville and Burlesque stars were happy to perform at these fund-raisers, often producing shows which money could not buy. This c. 1925 photograph advertises a "juvenile aquatic sports and social" to be held at Glasser's.

As a courtesy, Glasser would carry mail across the Lake to and from Nolans Point, where he regularly picked up supplies. Glasser applied and was granted a summer post office in 1933. The postal service rejected the name Northwood, as there were five others in the United States. The name Henderson was also turned down. The postal authorities noted that most mail came c/o Glasser and suggested that name. Here is Glasser's Pavilion and dock, *c.* 1925.

William Glasser served as the postmaster of Glasser from 1933 until retiring in 1949. His son, William Glasser, Jr., served from 1950 until 1972. In 1954, Glasser became a year-round post office. After Glasser sold the store in 1958 it was renamed the Northwood Inn. Father and son are seen here after the post office moved to a building next door. The post office is still located here today.

The closest Hopatcong has come to a real "downtown" was River Styx of the 1930s to 1950s. Three separate rows of stores lined a small section of River Styx Road, with additional stores located closer to the bridge where the Grotto Restaurant is located today. The earliest of these, seen in this c. 1930 photograph, was located at the corner of River Styx Road and Lakeside Boulevard.

These stores were owned for many years by local realtor Theodore Rossy, who maintained his office here. Rossy was very active in the development of Hopatcong, operating here from the 1920s through the 1950s. In the late 1940s, Rossy converted several of the stores to apartments, as they remain today. The Boulevard Restaurant currently occupies the corner store.

BUSINESS SECTION OF RIVER STYX ON LAKE HOPATCONG, N.J.

Proceeding down River Styx Road were three more stores. For many years, the larger store next to Feurstein's Tavern was Feurstein's Grocery, becoming Van's Market during the 1950s and early 1960s, and then the Mediterranean Market. The middle building served as the Hopatcong Post Office from 1934 into the 1950s. The building on the left in this *c.* 1940 photograph is the only one which still stands. It is currently Lake's Edge Florist.

BUSINESS CENTER RIVER STYX RD. HOPATCONG, N.J.

Across the street, now a parking area for the Hudson Maxim School, were an early dance hall, later a game arcade, and other stores. This 1947 photograph shows Jimmy's Arcade and Lunch Bar, as well as River Styx's own five-and-dime store. These stores were torn down in the late 1950s.

Located by the River Styx Bridge, the River Styx Casino featured refreshments, dancing, bathing, and boating during the early 1920s. Its slogan was "The Place to Meet." The Venice Restaurant, the Yellow Bowl, and the Nut Club would occupy the site before it burned in September 1933. Sheppie's would be built on the site in 1940.

In the years following World War II, the center of social life at the Lake was River Styx. An assortment of establishments developed on both sides of the River Styx Bridge, offering a variety of music, dancing, and drinking venues. Places such as Sheppie's, the Log Cabin, Rainbow Inn, Kay's, Feurstein's, and the bar at the Bon Air Lodge made River Styx a popular spot on weekends. The best-remembered place is the Mad House.

Located at the River Styx Bridge, the Mad House opened in the 1920s during Prohibition. Located at a major resort, it is not surprising that the Mad House and several other Lake establishments are purported to have been speakeasies. In 1931, the name was changed to Andy's Pavilion and it was moved closer to the water. Following Prohibition's end in 1932, it became a tavern, and in 1935 changed its name back to the Mad House. It featured two bars (the lower one seen in this 1950s photograph), live music, and dancing.

In a scene similar to some Jersey Shore towns today, the 1950s saw the River Styx Bridge a buzz of activity as revelers tried to determine where the best music and crowd was to be found. One of the favorite mid-week activities at the Lake was the Mad House's famous Amateur Night every Tuesday. The Mad House burned in 1970 and the site has remained vacant.

Sheppie's opened in the spring of 1940. The original structure, as seen in this photograph, had a wonderful, Art Deco design. Featuring the "glass bar," a Hammond organ, and the Empire and Tropical rooms, Sheppie's was a favorite during the 1940s and 1950s. It's "Musical Quiz" every Wednesday was an institution for many vacationers at the Lake.

A happy bar crowd is seen in this c. 1950 photograph. Northwood's own Helen Jungfer was a favorite at the Hammond organ at Sheppie's for many years. In 1956, Sheppie's became Rachel's and featured Chinese food, as well as Italian food and pizza. The interior was heavily damaged by a winter fire in 1964 and needed serious renovations. In recent years, The Upper Deck, Savannah's, and now the Tidal Wave have operated here.

In 1925, Anton Feurstein opened Feurstein's as a grocery, delicatessen, lunch room, and small hotel. In the 1930s, when his brother William opened a separate grocery two doors down, Anton's business became a restaurant, bar, liquor store, and rooming house. Feurstein's created quite a stir in 1940 by installing one of the first televisions at Lake Hopatcong.

In 1933, two partners, James Ryan and John Coyle, opened a Chinese-American restaurant in River Styx. Known as the Log Cabin Tea Garden, their advertisement listed lunch at 50¢ and dinner at 75¢. In addition, they featured dances on Saturdays and Sundays.

In the late 1940s, future Hopatcong mayor Nick Gentile's Martinique was a popular spot in Sperry Springs. It included a soda fountain and luncheonette, as well as a cocktail bar with live entertainment. As seen in this 1940s photograph, its waterfront location attracted a crowd.

Nick Gentile sold the Martinique in 1955 and bought Kranich's Hardware Store ("Store of a Million Items") in River Styx. The Martinique would continue as a cocktail lounge through the 1980s. It is now a private residence.

FOUNTAIN INN – LAKE HOPATCONG, N.J.
OPEN ALL YEAR – PHONE HOPATCONG 52.

AT THE LANDING
TURN LEFT ONE MILE
TO THE FOUNTAIN.

FOUNTAIN·BAR

BEER

Spur

Located on the corner of Brooklyn-Stanhope Road and Lakeside Boulevard, the Fountain Inn was popular with folks visiting Hopatcong State Park. Featuring a snack bar, soda fountain, and cocktail lounge, it operated from the 1930s through the 1950s on the site of the old Brooklyn Hotel. The Fountain Inn is a private residence today.

Le Beaulieu

Lakeside Boulevard
HOPATCONG, N.J.

Following the fire at the Fairways Bowling Alley, the Flintlock Restaurant opened on the site in 1963, built in a rustic style. Le Beaulieu followed the Flintlock and was very popular in the late 1960s and early 1970s. The Governor's Inn and the current occupant, Changes Night Club, have enlarged the original structure.

111

PHONE HOP. 8-0043
LANDING, N. J.

-nothing takes the place of MILK

_____195____

M_____

To ROY STONE, Dr.

All accounts must be paid weekly.　　　　Route No._____

Balance		$

From	to	Inc.

_____Quarts of Milk @ _____cts. qt.　$_____

_____Quarts of Milk @ _____cts. qt.　$_____

_____of Pot Cheese @ _____cts. pt.　$_____

_____of Cream @ _____cts.　　　$_____

_____cts.　　　$_____

Stone's Dairy was a landmark in Hopatcong. From the 1920s through the 1960s, Hiram Stone, and later his son Roy, operated this full-service dairy on Lakeside Boulevard, delivering milk and other products. An ice cream parlor was added in the 1930s. Just to the front of their property sat the Hopatcong Jail, a stone structure used in Hopatcong's early days, usually to sober up a wayward party-goer. The building is still owned by the Borough.

As growth escalated during the 1960s in Hopatcong, additional stores opened to serve what was becoming an increasingly year-round population. This 1963 photograph shows what is now Garden Cleaners on Lakeside Boulevard. In the window is a sign wishing Hopatcong resident Janet Adams good luck in the 1963 Miss America Pageant. The store has since been expanded and other stores added.

Seven
Lazy Days of Summer (and Winter)

Recreation has played a key role in Hopatcong's first century. Whether it was tour boats (as seen in this 1930s photograph taken in River Styx) or River Styx's miniature golf course, vacationers needed ways to have fun. With the end of World War II, it became clear that tourism in Hopatcong had changed. Although some hotels reopened after World War II, and the final hotel did not close until the 1970s, Lake Hopatcong's era as a hotel resort had really ended in the 1930s. The Lake's communities, including Hopatcong, were evolving into a different type of resort. The majority of summer residents now were second home-owners or renters. Yet, during both periods, a host of recreational activities kept folks coming back season after season.

Water carnivals were popular events during much of Hopatcong's first 100 years. This early carnival sponsored by the West Side Association featured a steam launch race, angler's casting tournament, bicycle race, and baseball-throwing contest, plus the ever popular fireworks with prizes for best shore and boat decorations. Established in 1894, the West Side Association looked after the interests of the west shore.

This 1922 water carnival attracted quite a crowd to the River Styx Casino. The River Styx Bridge provided the perfect spot for a bird's-eye view.

Water carnivals, centering around Glasser's Pavilion, were a yearly event at Northwood. An aquatic pie-eating contest is shown in this *c.* 1950 carnival.

A photograph of the 1947 Northwood Carnival shows a tube race in progress. These carnivals were a favorite amongst the kids.

Swimming has, of course, always been a focus of the Lake life. This *c.* 1905 photograph was taken in Byram Cove. While swimsuits have certainly changed over the years, the enjoyment has stayed the same.

Fishing has always been popular at the Lake. Since 1946, the Knee Deep Club has done much to increase interest and awareness in fishing at the Lake and has sponsored a very successful stocking program. Interestingly, only catfish, sunfish, and yellow perch are considered native to the Lake. This *c.* 1912 photograph, taken at the Hotel Durban dock, shows a good day's catch.

116

Beginning with the dugout canoes of the Lenape people, Lake Hopatcong's history and development have been closely tied to the boats that plied its waters. Naphtha launches, similar to the one Mrs. Van Wagonen is driving in this *c.* 1900 photograph, were the first power pleasure craft on the Lake. When introduced in the 1890s, they stunned spectators with their awesome 8–10 mph speed.

Boats powered by internal combustion engines, such as Palmers and Fay-Bowens, succeeded the relatively unsafe naphtha launches. This idyllic 1916 photo shows the Gibb family out for a pleasant ride on the Lake.

In addition to power craft, rowboats, sailboats, canoes, and variations of the three have all been popular over the years. This *c.* 1912 photograph shows a canoe race in progress. Hopatcong's Dudley Gessler, of Boulders Cottage, is the gentleman in the rear.

While early competitions on the Lake often revolved around power boats, sailing has been the predominant form of racing since World War II. Sail boat regattas, like the one seen in this 1930s photograph, remain a favorite weekend event at the Lake.

The late Fred Jacoby, a Hopatcong summer resident, was a champion outboard racer and world record holder. His inspiration to become involved with race boats came after his first visit to the Lake in 1928. Fred is pictured here with his wife, Tem, who still resides in Hopatcong.

Fred Jacoby Boat Works, run by Fred's father, was located in North Bergen. Fred competed in outboard racing competitions around the United States. A surviving Jacoby racing boat now resides at Northwood Boat Works.

The World's Fastest Racing Outboard

Built by FRED JACOBY BOAT WORKS

- Class X Record—1 mile, 78.121 m.p.h.
  Made by Bedford Davie

- Class X Record—5 mile, 61.392 m.p.h.
  Made by Clinton Ferguson

- Marathon Record—52.53 m.p.h.
  Made by Harry N. Birdsall

119

In 1918, Mayor Theodore Gessler led the effort to organize the Lake Hopatcong Country Club. Built on the old, 110-acre Brown farm, play began in 1919 on the 3,460-yard, nine-hole course. The old barn was converted into the clubhouse as seen in this 1930s photograph. The adjoining Davis farm was acquired, and in 1931 the course expanded to 18 holes. In 1959, the course sold land to the Hopatcong Board of Education for the high school and the course reverted to nine holes.

Announcing - - -

NEW GREEN FEES

LAKE HOPATCONG COUNTRY CLUB

—— 18 Holes ——

Golfers Welcome

Week Days	$1.50
Sat., Sun., Holidays	2.00
Weekly	10.00
Monthly	25.00
Season, Men	50.00
Season, Women	25.00
Caddy Fees, 18 Holes	80c.

The course was too hilly for power carts and too taxing for many golfers (one hole was affectionately known as "Cardiac Hill"). It operated until the 1970s. After being closed a few years, the Borough of Hopatcong acquired the course in 1976. Athletic fields now exist on the old fairways and the clubhouse serves as the Hopatcong Civic Center. Greens Fees have sure changed from this 1932 advertisement.

Fairways opened on Lakeside Boulevard in 1939 and in 1940 it was probably the first location in Hopatcong to have air conditioning. Along with four bowling alleys, it featured shuffleboard, dining, and dancing. By 1948, Fairways boasted 12 alleys, and in 1949 it hosted the New Jersey Bowling Championships. Fairways was destroyed by fire in 1961 and replaced by a restaurant. Changes Night Club now operates on the site.

Located on Brooklyn-Stanhope Road, about .25 miles from Hopatcong State Park, the Hopatcong Bear Farm and Zoo operated during the early 1960s. In addition to animals, there were refreshments and rides. The site has been vacant since the zoo closed.

The Maxim Park Yacht Club was organized in 1914 by some of the Lake's best-known residents. The brain child of L.A. Morey, its first officers included Hudson Maxim and Rex Beach (one of America's most popular authors of the 1910s and 1920s). Maxim donated a perpetual lease for the land on Cow Tongue Point, along with the old Henderson Hotel building, which was on the property.

Dedicated to the improvement of Lake Hopatcong, the club's members were largely responsible for securing telephone service around the Lake. By September 1914, the club had 200 members and had begun work on its clubhouse. It opened on August 14, 1915, with a parade of 75 boats. Although the club closed in the 1920s, the clubhouse survives as one of the Lake's most picturesque homes.

After World War II, a group of friends began to meet at the Lake, usually at the Bon Air Lodge. In this era, Jews, like many other groups, were restricted from most clubs, so the group decided to organize their own. When plans to build on Halsey Island fell apart, they acquired Hillcrest and opened the Garden State Yacht Club in 1951. The club prospered, growing in membership, adding a pool, railway, and other amenities. Disaster struck on December 6, 1984, when fire destroyed the clubhouse. To its credit, the club persevered and built a new clubhouse on the site in 1986.

HUDSON GUILD FARM, NEAR BEAR POND, N.J.
(Flo + Bill, Pubs.)

On the Stanhope-Sparta Road lies Hudson Guild Farm, established as a non-sectarian camp in 1917 by the Hudson Guild of New York City, a well-known settlement house with socialist-type ideals. The Hudson Guild took city kids to the country to teach them the essentials of farming, while also offering traditional camp activities. In recent years, the farm was a retreat for senior citizens from the city. The farm was just recently sold and, happily, it appears the buyer plans on keeping it intact. This c. 1940 photograph shows the old McCroy mansion, the main building for the farm.

During Lake Hopatcong's early years, land was readily available and several summer camps were established. The two largest camps were located in Hopatcong. Camp Alhtaha was opened by the Paterson Council of Boy Scouts in 1929. It was located in Byram Cove, then a remote part of the Lake with no road access. This c. 1930 photograph shows the campers in front of the mess hall.

Camp Alhtaha is seen from the Lake c. 1930, with the mess hall constructed on a rock ledge. Stairs lead down to the 100-foot-long dock. Camp Alhtaha operated for about 10 years. Following World War II, the land was sold to a group of public works engineers from New York City. The mess hall and two other buildings were converted to residences and still survive today.

Camp Tegawitha was established in 1925 as a Catholic girl's camp on the west shore, just north of Hopatcong State Park. The camp's cabins are seen in this c. 1940 photograph. Tegawitha had a boathouse and swimming area on the Lake. It was the last camp to operate at the Lake, closing in the early 1970s. The buildings have been leveled and the site remains vacant today.

Witt's Training Camp was established in 1931 at Sperry Springs by Charles Witten. Boys who came to the camp learned to box, swim, and dive. Although the boxing camp only operated formally for a few seasons, Charlie Witten lived in Sperry Springs through the 1970s. Witten was very generous with his time and taught many a local youngster to swim, dive, and box. Charlie, a former amateur flyweight, is seen at the camp in this 1931 photograph.

Throughout Hopatcong's first century, winter sports on the Lake have been a popular pastime. This 1925 photograph shows a group of skate sailors. Skate sailing reached its peak during the 1920s and 1930s.

During the early years, the frozen Lake had to be shared with the ice harvesters, so some areas were off limits for recreation. Ice fishing, as seen in this *c.* 1920 photograph, remains a popular hobby at the Lake.

There were well-organized hockey leagues on the Lake. The area in front of the Bon Air Lodge in River Styx was a regular location for hockey games during the 1920s and 1930s. This c. 1940 photograph shows the team from Sheppie's. Sheppie's Blue Devils were co-champions of the 1941 New Jersey Hockey League.

During the Lake's peak resort years of the 1920s, winter carnivals were scheduled. These carnivals, covered by the New York papers, would bring publicity to the Lake during the off season and draw people back to the Lake to participate and watch. The 1926 carnival reportedly brought 15,000 people to the Lake. Always a part of ice carnivals, ice boating (as seen in this 1920s photograph) has long been a popular winter activity at the Lake.

Annual River Styx Reunion

LAKE HOPATCONG, N. J.

Friday Evening, October 19th, 1923

HOTEL PENNSYLVANIA, NEW YORK CITY

Music by Castle Club Orchestra of Columbia University

Subscription Three Dollars Per Couple

DODD COSTER
100 Haven Avenue
New York City

JACK WIESING
46 Lincoln Street
Jersey City, N. J

As the 1960s dawned, change was on the horizon. The first sections of a new interstate highway were being completed near Hopatcong. Few at the time realized the profound changes that Route 80 and the increased accessibility it brought would have on the community. Hopatcong grew from a population of 1,100 in 1950 to over 15,000 in 1980. The last vestiges of the resort era faded and Hopatcong became a year-round community.

Hold on for the next 100 years . . .